Redouté Flowers
COLORING BOOK

Charlene Tarbox

DOVER PUBLICATIONS, INC.
Mineola, New York

NOTE

The flowers in this book are carefully rendered after paintings by Pierre-Joseph Redouté (1759–1840). In this collection of floral illustrations, one can truly appreciate Redouté's botanical artistry. Redouté, perhaps best known for his breathtaking paintings of roses, created many of his works while employed by Empress Josephine. The floral plates are arranged alphabetically according to common name. The captions also include the flower's scientific name. Each flower is shown in color on the inside front and back covers.

Bibliographical Note

Redouté Flowers Coloring Book is a new work, first published by
Dover Publications, Inc., in 1998.

International Standard Book Number

ISBN-13: 978-0-486-40055-6
ISBN-10: 0-486-40055-7

Manufactured in the United States by LSC Communications
40055715   2017
www.doverpublications.com

1. Alpine Brier Rose *(Rosa pendulina vulgaris)*

2. Althaea, Rose-of-Sharon (*Hibiscus syriacus*)

3. Amaryllis *(Hippeastrum puniceum)*

4. Anemone (*Anemone coronaria*)

5. Apple Blossoms *(Malus pumila)*

6. Bindweed, Dwarf Morning-Glory *(Convolvulus tricolor)*

7. Burgundy Rose (*Rosa centifolia parvifolia*)

8. Campion (*Lychnis coronata*)

9. China Aster (*Callistephus chinensis*)

10. Christmas Rose and Carnations *(Helleborus niger* and *Dianthus caryophyllus)*

11. Dahlia *(Dahlia pinnata)*

12. Dillenia *(Hibbertia scandens)*

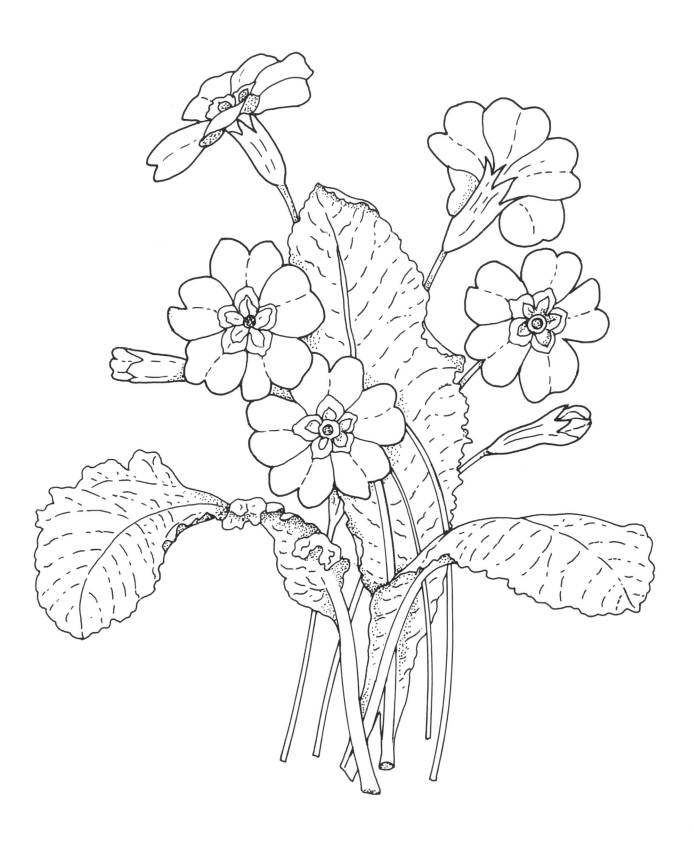

13. English Primrose *(Primula vulgaris)*

14. Enkianthus *(Enkianthus quinqueflorus)*

15. Gaillardia (*Gaillardia pulchella*)

16. Gentian *(Gentiana acaulis)*

17. Geranium (*Pelargonium daveyanum*)

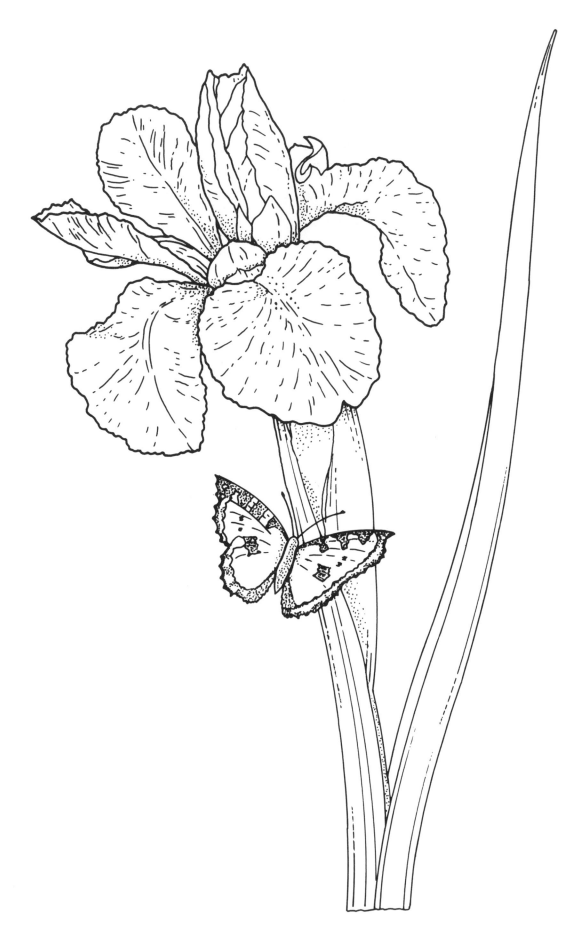

18. Iris *(Iris xiphium)*

19. Italian Damask Rose *(Rosa damascena italica)*

20. Marbled Rose (*Rosa gallica flore marmoreo*)

21. Narcissus / Daffodil hybrid (*Narcissus x incomparabilis*)

22. Peony (white form) *(Paeonia officinalis)*

23. Peony (deep pink form) *(Paeonia officinalis)*

24. Rose of Love (*Rosa gallica pumila*)

25. Rose of Orleans, French Rose (*Rosa gallica aurelianensis*)

26. Soft Rose *(Rosa mollis)*

27. Sweet Pea (*Lathyrus odoratus*)

28. Tea Rose (*Rosa odorata*)

29. Tulip (*Tulipa gesneriana*)

30. Wild Pansies, Field Pansies *(Viola tricolor)*